Beauty AND THE BEAST rap

Written by Sonja Dunn
Illustrated by Susan Darrach

MOONSTONE PRESS

Of all the old tales
This is not the least
It's the enchanting story
Of Beauty and the Beast

Beauty didn't ask for
Fancy clothes
All covered up
With buttons and bows

She didn't stand
At the mirror
And pose
Or yearn for handsome
Romeos

She just asked her father
"Do you suppose
That you could bring me
One red rose?"

One red
One red
One red rose

I said
One red
One red
One red rose

Her merchant father
Travelled wide
To distant countries
He would ride
To sell his goods
And buy some too
Silken cloth
Of brilliant hue

I said
Brilliant
Brilliant
Brilliant hue

And while his daughter
Beauty stayed
Behind at home
She daily played
Some chess
Some golf
Some tennis too

She hiked
She swam
She read
She drew

But both her sisters
She did find
Complained of being bored
And whined
While waiting for
Their merchant dad
To see what stuff
For them he had

When to their home
Their dad returned
His dreadful tale
Beauty soon learned
About a Beast's
Enchanted garden
And how this Beast
Would only pardon
Her dad from death
If he so chose

For stealing
One red
One red rose
One red
One red
One red rose

The Beast roared
"I will let you live
If in return to me you give
Your favoured one
Who does your duty
Your daughter fair
Whom you call Beauty
Don't plead with me
Don't beg and cry"
The fierce Beast growled
"Send her or die"

And that is how
It came to be
That this brave girl
No longer free
Lived with a Beast
And all his woes
And all because
Of one red rose
One red
One red
One red rose

At first the Beast
Was rough and rude
He paced and sneered
And tore his food
He snarled at all
Who dared come near
And only Beauty
Showed no fear

Beauty was kind
But she was firm
And soon the Beast
Began to learn
How to be gentle
Mild and fair
To all the beings
In his care

And from a creature
Wild and strange
She watched the Beast
Completely change

He brought her gifts
Of books and clothes
And precious things
Like one red rose
One red
One red
One red rose

I said
One red
One red
One red rose

Soon there was laughter
Everywhere
The garden bloomed
With roses fair
Roses
Roses
Roses fair

I said roses
Roses
Roses fair

When Beast and Beauty
Became best friends
The Beast said
He would make amends
Back to her family
She could go
On magic winds
That gently blow

Beauty came home
To joy and tears
The Beast's voice
Ringing in her ears
"Before the snow
Begins to fly
Return to me
Or I will die"

Beauty told her
Family how
The cruel Beast
Was friendly now
She gave them presents
He had sent
Together happy hours
They spent

But as the pleasant
Days sped by
She noticed
Snowflakes in the sky
And as with sorrow
Her heart burned
On magic winds
Beauty returned

She found the castle
Filled with gloom
There were no roses
Not one bloom
Not one
Not one
Not one bloom

When Beauty found
Her dear Beast friend
His life was coming
To an end
The Beast lay
Dying in repose
And on his breast
Was one dead rose
One dead·
One dead
One dead rose

I said
One dead
One dead
One dead rose

"Dear Beast" she said
"I'm here you see
I have returned
As you asked me"

"Too late" he said
"The harm's been done
The spell has worked
And fate has won"

And when these words
The Beast had spoken
He closed his eyes
His heart was broken

Sad Beauty cried
In great despair
Her tears fell
On his face and hair
"Don't die and let
Our friendship end
I've grown to love you
Dearest friend"

She gently kissed
His paws and mane
How would she ever
Smile again?

And then a rainbow
Opened wide
A valiant prince
Stood by her side
The Beast had vanished
And instead
There stood a man
Whom she would wed

"You've saved my life
You gave me grace
Not only are you
Fair of face
But you have taught me
How to be
A gracious man
Because you see

Long years ago
A sage so wise
Enchanted me
With a disguise
A beast was I
Destined to be
Until someone
With love freed me

For once I was
A dreadful youth
Haughty, uncaring
And uncouth
Truly a beast
In human form

But now that's ceased
And all because
You kindly chose
To tame me
Thanks to
One red rose
One red
One red
One red rose

I said
One red
One red
One red rose"

Now you can guess
This story's end
Her Beast turned prince
Was her true friend
Their lives were peaceful
Ever after
They all lived on
In joy and laughter
I said joy
I said joy
I said joy and laughter

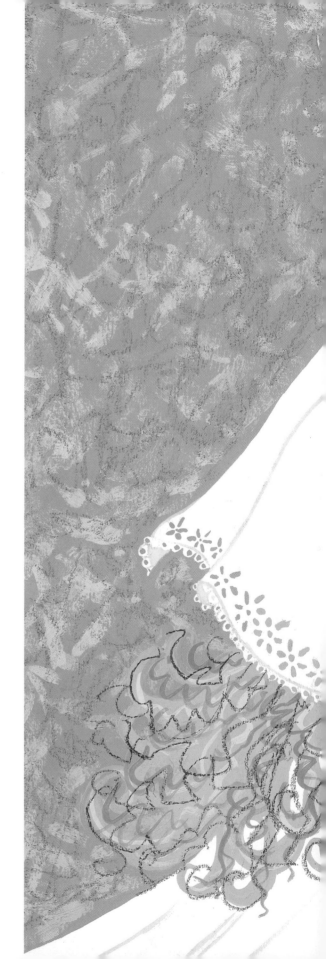

Author photograph courtesy Patrick McConnell, Etobicoke Life Newspaper.

Creative and production by Ceneda Creative Inc., Toronto.
Printed in Hong Kong.

Moonstone Press gratefully acknowledges the financial assistance of The Canada Council and the Ontario Arts Council.

Canadian Cataloguing in Publication Data

Dunn, Sonja, 1931-
    Beauty and the beast rap

Based on Beauty and the beast.
ISBN 0-920259-50-2

1. Children's poetry, Canadian (English).*
I. Darrach, Susan.   II. Title.

PS8557.U54856B4 1994   jC811'.54   C94-930198-1
P28.3.D85Be 1994

Moonstone Press
175 Brock Street
Goderich, Ontario
Canada N7A 1R4